Genesis

Genesis

Ashley R. Lumpkin

PPB

Pinnacle Place Books
Greensboro, NC
www.pinnacleplacebooks.com

Printed in the United States of America

Author Photo: Jackson Hall

ISBN: 978-1-7335818-5-1

For every Bible Study, Sunday School, and
Vacation Bible School teacher I had as a kid:

I'm pretty sure this is not what you had in
mind, but I did learn something.

TABLE OF CONTENTS

Creation

When your God, as you say, created the earth,
He made it a perfect sphere. Our calling it flat
had no bearing on the weight and round of it.
Our seeing an edge, did not make the horizon
any less arc.

And you call your daughter
your son.

Don't you see? She was made perfect this way.
Being born in a body that you call boy has
no bearing on the truth and girl of her. What
astronomy are you ignoring to preserve what has
always been a lie?

Centuries later there are those amongst us who
still believe in a flat earth - still require some
proof beyond all that we can see.

When your God, as you say, created the earth,
He said, "Let there be," and so it was. She
has said to us all, "This is who I am," and so it is.
And it is good.

**The Book of the Generations
of this Depression**

In the beginning was Helen
        who was sometimes Cynthia
        and sometimes Grace
And Helen begat my father
        and Cynthia begat his quick temper
        and Grace begat his smooth tongue
And his tongue begat him a line of women that wrapped around the
block
The block begat his drive to leave the city
The city begat the grief he carried with him
        (This is the grief that drug him to the bottom of the
        bottle)
And rock bottom begat the girl who believed that she could change
him
And change begat the beginning of their new life together
Which begat Kentucky
Which begat Wurzburg
Which begat Arizona
Which begat Virginia
Which begat a small town to settle down in that felt like dust tracks
on a road
And once the dust settled Cynthia reared back up in the blood line
        begat anger
        begat secrets
        begat a death knell tolling in the family photos
And the girl who believed in change once begat a ghost still in search
of her bones

Let x be the Bread
(or: communion is an equation we balance with heaven)

Memory, it seems, is a function of x.
We divide x by 2, and 5000 ghosts join us in
the living room. They scatter themselves in
predictable clusters; wait for us to plot the
curve; praise what we do here that they once
took for granted.

We halve $f(x)$ again, and my daughter hums as
she chews. The ghosts remember the miracle
of bread, multiplying and dividing in the same
instant - a function and its inverse moving
forward in real time.

The boy who provided the loaves to begin with
forgets all five by Passover. He does not look
my daughter in the eye. She reaches for her cup
of juice before we read the next scripture.

Thirst is a parallel function of bread - memory
a desperate craving for water. The apostles
gather at the fireplace and begin to dig a
well. They pause for a moment to calculate the
depth of our desire.

Let n be the number of ways the world can
leave us wanting. We search for our own limits
as n approaches the infinite. We pray for a
messiah that is also a mathematician. A cluster
of ghosts recalls the first time they saw Him
breaking bread.

My daughter smiles at her empty cup;
a book of sonnets falls from the shelf;

the boy remembers being a hero;
and n decreases a bit.

This is a function of memory - to take
a ghost and give it wings, and now 5000
seraphim sing a chorus in my living room.
Praise the water we find here. Praise these
angels of bread.

Messiah

let us begin with broken glass by the bathtub
shower running cold at three am
tennessee honey pooling in the seams between the tiles
it is one thing to know that alcoholism runs on both sides of the
bloodline
another to wake up bleeding and cold with bottle shards trapped in
the knots of my hair
in one version of the story it's a wakeup call
let's say wake up calls are for sunday mornings
what should i do with the bible i keep tucked beneath the sink

let's say the bible is a true story
that jesus did turn water to wine
the wine then transubstantiated into his own blood
what am i then but a parable
the bathtub a baptismal pool
the glass a crown of thorns i placed upon my own head
what is the true cost of blasphemy
maybe a hangover
a few scars

let's say my grandmother taught me the best hangover cure the
morning i turned twelve years old
after a shot of jack but before the birthday party
that the only two things she knows about being an alcoholic are that
it's bad to be one
and that they drink alone

let's say the house is filled with grandchildren that don't ask any
questions
what should i do when being obedient also means bending the rules
call my grandma john the baptist
who also lived on wild honey
also made the way for the coming messiah

what is being born again if not waking up in a hospital
everyone but me crying and calling on the son of god
in one version of the story it's a wake up call
let's say wake up calls are for twenty-third birthdays
what should i do with a suicide attempt that starts out as a good time

it is one thing to actually have an addiction
another to need a convenient excuse on a saturday night when the
bartender takes my keys before i've had the first sip
let's say my drink of choice is the entire bottle
that i'm grandma's most faithful disciple
that being sober any night of the week sometimes feels like a kind of
betrayal

let's say i'm the only one in my family for whom drinking is still a
choice
that i'm building a life out of rebounding all the times i've chosen
wrong
that i know the first step on the road to redemption is admitting that i
might have a problem
but i am still on step zero
getting black out drunk and apologizing

there is a school of thought that teaches jesus was addicted to giving
forgiveness
that he surrounded himself with sinners just to get his next fix
what should i do on the days i am trapped between being an addict
and the addiction

i swear
i am so drunk and empty i feel like a child of god

Good Earth

The ones that smell like good earth and sunlight,
spread wide and green and spilling out – taking all the
space on the kitchen table before they even come out
the bag – those are the collards that are good enough
to be served at Grandma's funeral.

*Remember the scripture? How God wants a church without
spot or wrinkle? Well, we don't want to find no spots in our
supper either.*

So, we search the leaves, one at a time, picking away
the black spots that do not serve us, then rip all the
green good that's left clean away from the stem.

*Some folks will tell you to save them stems. I say, Sunday
dinner ain't time to make do.*

And there they are. A little changed, but not at all
worse for the wear – ready for the first rinse and soak,
the first good singing to.

*You got to sing to them collards. Make 'em want to do you
right.*

So, we sing all the verses to Amazing Grace. Slow,
just the way Grandma likes. And no one cries because
then you'll taste the sadness in the pot liquor. But
everyone takes a turn getting their hands in the sink.

Each takes a turn checking in on the men, in the
next room talking bills and burial plots. The minister
asking questions about the funeral, and the greens
in the kitchen just holy and clean. And the job of
cutting the collards should go to the oldest daughter,

but she's in the bedroom with the shades all drawn.

You got to get the bundles tight. Loose collards don't settle, just like loose women, and I won't have either in my house.

So, we all take turns, stacking the leaves, rolling them full and ready to chop. Even the youngest of the cousins has a turn at the cutting board, until the whole batch of them is ready for the second wash.

That's the secret. Soak 'em again. Right before they go in the pot. In water and vinegar and a little salt. Everything else is up to the heat.

Everything else is small talk and steaming the dresses, waiting for the morning and the caravan to come – to carry the pots from the kitchen to church and moan over how good these greens really are. But only after the service. After the men carry the casket around to the back of the church, and we sing up some more of that grace. Return Grandma to the good earth.

This is Just to Say
after William Carlos Williams

i wrote in the margins
of the family bible,
laid open on the coffee
table.

i know that we're to
only inscribe when
someone new joins
us. or departs.

forgive me.

i found the notes
from the sunday
grandpop preached
his first sermon.

i did not get to meet him.
i wanted to say amen.

**for absuers who consider jewelry/
when the rainbow is not enough**

the story goes
that after the flood god placed a rainbow center sky
said all this beauty is my promise not to flood the earth
again
when you see it
take comfort
perhaps even joy that the thunder's bark is worse than its
bite
and you have survived the worst of it
the rainbow means survival
means mercy
means praise the god who gives us grace after he destroys
us

and noah's wife is mentioned just once in the scripture
before the ark
before even noah
she is named amongst her brothers
and they too are not heard from again
i wonder how long after giving the dowry noah began to
talk of destruction
telling his wife that her people would die and that they
would deserve it
calling himself a savior while calling her family sin

the story goes
my mother has four siblings
and i still don't know each of their names
sometime after the wedding my father cut off all
communication
built the two of them a home
then called his vices two by two
a little addiction
a little adultery

and mom there to clean up the mess
but they never tell you in sunday school that the ark was
filled with animal waste
so mom will never tell you that my dad is full of shit

the story goes
that after the hospital he placed a bracelet around her wrist
said all this beauty is my promise not to break your jaw
again
when you see it take comfort
perhaps even joy that you have seen both bark and bite
and learned not to earn it
isn't that what it means to fall in love with a vengeful god
to worship a man who looks at his rage and calls the
violence holy

i sit in the back of bible study
weighing the difference between threat and promise
what it means to call a rainbow beautiful on the backs of
drowning bodies
consider a god who offers jewelry to cover a broken
horizon

the story goes
that with the promise god also gave a warning
said the next time we went too far with free will
the flood would become a fire
my father held mom's hand the entire ride home from the
hospital
squeezed it when we passed a cemetery
then again when we passed a funeral home
i consider a broken jawbone as kindling for cremation
what wouldn't you endure to hold back the burning

would you ignore your family's phone calls
give the man three kids
could you handle being afraid for so long you started to call
it faith
wear the bracelet to church on sundays
call the damn thing beautiful

Hephzibah

i.

When the name of the town that you grow up in is a
Biblical character no one remembers, you start to view
the moment you leave it as a kind of second coming.
Whether school or the service is personal savior to
rapture you out of its small and simple, the only thing
of which you are certain is you do not intend to look
back. Just ask Lot's wife - the pillar of salt you lean
on when you wax nostalgic - if she would like another
chance to run away from home. Anywhere else is
already better than the time lapse of this town, which
is all the world the old folks here will ever get to see.
When you say Venice, or Madrid, or even some place
like Atlanta, they hear the distant corners of a reaching
outer space. You, some type of alien at odds with the
slow down too stubborn to know a good thing when
you got one.

ii.

You're a small-town girl with a big city heart pumping
"go" to the swell at the tips of your fingers. They don't
understand why staying here would feel like a life of
suicide; how you have already started to suffocate at
the thought of not living your dreams; how you have
seen the shades of hopelessness that people settle into.
All they ever seem to do is work and wait to die.

iii.

There are just two cemeteries here. Both of them
running out of space. The gravestones read an
apocryphal reference to all of the things willingly
forgotten. Your one-way ticket from here reads to
them like the Gospel of Judas. You are Jezebel lusting
after a city that is not your own. You do not know

where it is. Trust you will know it when you get there.
It will settle into your empty spaces as quiet as a psalm;
or a secret; or passage of scripture overlooked every
time you have been in church.

iv.
Jesus
only returned
to Jerusalem
when He knew it was His time to die.
And you are no messiah,
just a girl
trying to make home.

Once More

and yet once more, i am on my knees, begging
a man to make me holy – making communion
from his frail body and all the ways i can cull an
amen. and isn't that sacrifice? isn't that worship?
isn't that what heaven would have of me? that i
offer up my own body as atonement for my sin?

and yet once more, i consider sin and what i
have called forgiveness. how i prayed without fail
nearly four thousand days and each prayer went
unanswered. each smile won from across a room
would turn my stomach in on itself. i became
jonah and whale and sweltering sea with no
shoreline to return to.

still i swam. still i prayed. still i allowed myself
belief, until the first time i allowed myself held
by delicate hands – a voice that cried out holy
but did not call for blood.

and yet once more, he shakes the heavens, and
i do not feel the quaking. instead, i feel my own
faith settle at the base of my spine. she takes my
hand, and the whale finds joy in its expanse of
water.

who now to pray to if not a god who loves me
as i am? what now to worship if not my own
body for the first time? and then, once more.

Firmament

It began with Pluto, once ninth in
line in my wonted sky, a comfort,
even if unseen – exiled from its proper
place as planet. And now science asserts
that earth has called a new moon
into its gravity. I suppose if heaven
can change, there is hope for me.

The Iron Skillet is
the Philosopher's Stone

Praise the family that gathers – even if just for this
moment – to find a Sabbath from our weary journeys
in the sameness of our skin. We are a family of
travelers. A family of runners. A family of skeletons
trapped inside closets – all melanin and mishap
boiled over in the blood, but on Sundays we get it
near right.

And not everyone goes to temple these days – not
since Ron found a bullet inside his son's mouth – but
here we still bow our heads. Here, we are grateful
for black girl alchemy: how they make miracles from
pepper and rice; how the sizzle and spill of a too-big
pot will be manna and magic if anything at all; how
everyone still comes home.

And Ruth isn't here. Or Helen. Or Gladys. But
there's okra, and cornbread, and deep-fried catfish so
good we can still hear them laugh when our cousins
sigh and ask for more. When Tony comes in late and
a little too drunk to wear the honor of our last name
well, we still offer him the head of the table since
Grandpa has long since closed his eyes. And there
are no questions, just grace, and God, how good it is
to be here.

Praise this family. These stories. This heritage in the
heat. This seasoned steel of our sharpened spines,
every Sunday we choose to come together after a
lifetime of reasons to run away. Praise this table and
the heart we stewed up here. How it will always fold
around our bodies to deliver us warm and full.

Mythomaniac

i know there is no place in heaven for liars - no
matter the reason they hide the truth - especially
if their own reflections are told more fiction than
anyone else. listen. i haven't prayed in a while.
omniscience is an obvious foe of deceit, but i
did build this altar. to whomever up there is in
charge of loopholes. here, the ring that alex gave
me the night of our fist kiss, a suicide note, some
peppermint oil, a tiny piece of sandstone - every
tangible reminder of times i found mercy i did
not think i deserved. i lit the candle placed in my
hand the first time a ceremony said i belonged,
and i cried without any words. all these, the most
honest parts of me - offered, i guess, as sacrifice.
i would tell you what i'm praying for, but i do not
want to lie.

Temple

she says come as you are
but i still try to bring only my best
black suit pressed to crisp perfection
ready to offer praise

she says
i see the whole of you
beneath all that finish
i swear you can come as you are

i bring her my broken
she reads from a holy book
bring her my shame
she offers a song

i try to sing
and the melody changes
the choir a fortress of empty stares
a clear bowl shakes on the altar
and water spills to the floor

she said
come as you are
but when i arrived
she had closed the door

End Notes

While this book is not intended to provide commentary
on Scripture per se, it is worth knowing that several
pieces are more readily understood with some
knowledge of the stories to which the poems allude.
Here, will you find that context, taken from the English
Standard Version of the Bible.

Contents

Genesis 1: 1 - 31
(Creation)

[1] In the beginning, God created the heavens and the earth.

[2] The earth was without form and void, and darkness was over the face of the deep. And the Spirit of God was hovering over the face of the waters.

[3] And God said, "Let there be light," and there was light.

[4] And God saw that the light was good. And God separated the light from the darkness.

[5] God called the light Day, and the darkness he called Night. And there was evening and there was morning, the first day.

[6] And God said, "Let there be an expanse in the midst of the waters, and let it separate the waters from the waters."

[7] And God made the expanse and separated the waters that were under the expanse from the waters that were above the expanse. And it was so.

[8] And God called the expanse Heaven. And there was evening and there was morning, the second day.

[9] And God said, "Let the waters under the heavens be gathered together into one place, and let the dry land appear." And it was so.

[10] God called the dry land Earth, and the waters that

were gathered together he called Seas. And God saw that it was good.

[11] And God said, "Let the earth sprout vegetation, plants yielding seed, and fruit trees bearing fruit in which is their seed, each according to its kind, on the earth." And it was so.

[12] The earth brought forth vegetation, plants yielding seed according to their own kinds, and trees bearing fruit in which is their seed, each according to its kind. And God saw that it was good.

[13] And there was evening and there was morning, the third day.

[14] And God said, "Let there be lights in the expanse of the heavens to separate the day from the night. And let them be for signs and for seasons, and for days and years,

[15] and let them be lights in the expanse of the heavens to give light upon the earth." And it was so.

[16] And God made the two great lights—the greater light to rule the day and the lesser light to rule the night—and the stars.

[17] And God set them in the expanse of the heavens to give light on the earth,

[18] to rule over the day and over the night, and to separate the light from the darkness. And God saw that it was good.

[19] And there was evening and there was morning, the fourth day.

[20] And God said, "Let the waters swarm with swarms of living creatures, and let birds fly above the earth across the expanse of the heavens."

[21] So God created the great sea creatures and every living creature that moves, with which the waters swarm, according to their kinds, and every winged bird according to its kind. And God saw that it was good.

[22] And God blessed them, saying, "Be fruitful and multiply and fill the waters in the seas, and let birds multiply on the earth."
[23] And there was evening and there was morning, the fifth day.

[24] And God said, "Let the earth bring forth living creatures according to their kinds—livestock and creeping things and beasts of the earth according to their kinds." And it was so.

[25] And God made the beasts of the earth according to their kinds and the livestock according to their kinds, and everything that creeps on the ground according to its kind. And God saw that it was good.

[26] Then God said, "Let us make man in our image, after our likeness. And let them have dominion over the fish of the sea and over the birds of the heavens and over the livestock and over all the earth and over every creeping thing that creeps on the earth."

[27] So God created man in his own image,
    in the image of God he created him;
    male and female he created them.

[28] And God blessed them. And God said to them, "Be

fruitful and multiply and fill the earth and subdue it, and have dominion over the fish of the sea and over the birds of the heavens and over every living thing that moves on the earth."

[29] And God said, "Behold, I have given you every plant yielding seed that is on the face of all the earth, and every tree with seed in its fruit. You shall have them for food.

[30] And to every beast of the earth and to every bird of the heavens and to everything that creeps on the earth, everything that has the breath of life, I have given every green plant for food." And it was so.

[31] And God saw everything that he had made, and behold, it was very good. And there was evening and there was morning, the sixth day.

Matthew 14: 13 - 21

(Let x be the bread)

¹³ Now when Jesus heard this, he withdrew from there in a boat to a desolate place by himself. But when the crowds heard it, they followed him on foot from the towns.

¹⁴ When he went ashore he saw a great crowd, and he had compassion on them and healed their sick.

¹⁵ Now when it was evening, the disciples came to him and said, "This is a desolate place, and the day is now over; send the crowds away to go into the villages and buy food for themselves."

¹⁶ But Jesus said, "They need not go away; you give them something to eat."

¹⁷ They said to him, "We have only five loaves here and two fish."

¹⁸ And he said, "Bring them here to me."

¹⁹ Then he ordered the crowds to sit down on the grass, and taking the five loaves and the two fish, he looked up to heaven and said a blessing. Then he broke the loaves and gave them to the disciples, and the disciples gave them to the crowds.

²⁰ And they all ate and were satisfied. And they took up twelve baskets full of the broken pieces left over.

²¹ And those who ate were about five thousand men, besides women and children.

Genesis 7:10 - 9:17
(for abusers who consider jewelry)

[10] And after seven days the waters of the flood came upon the earth.

[11] In the six hundredth year of Noah's life, in the second month, on the seventeenth day of the month, on that day all the fountains of the great deep burst forth, and the windows of the heavens were opened.

[12] And rain fell upon the earth forty days and forty nights.

[13] On the very same day Noah and his sons, Shem and Ham and Japheth, and Noah's wife and the three wives of his sons with them entered the ark,

[14] they and every beast, according to its kind, and all the livestock according to their kinds, and every creeping thing that creeps on the earth, according to its kind, and every bird, according to its kind, every winged creature.

[15] They went into the ark with Noah, two and two of all flesh in which there was the breath of life.

[16] And those that entered, male and female of all flesh, went in as God had commanded him. And the LORD shut him in.

[17] The flood continued forty days on the earth. The waters increased and bore up the ark, and it rose high above the earth.

[18] The waters prevailed and increased greatly on the

earth, and the ark floated on the face of the waters.

[19] And the waters prevailed so mightily on the earth that all the high mountains under the whole heaven were covered.

[20] The waters prevailed above the mountains, covering them fifteen cubits[d] deep.

[21] And all flesh died that moved on the earth, birds, livestock, beasts, all swarming creatures that swarm on the earth, and all mankind.

[22] Everything on the dry land in whose nostrils was the breath of life died.

[23] He blotted out every living thing that was on the face of the ground, man and animals and creeping things and birds of the heavens. They were blotted out from the earth. Only Noah was left, and those who were with him in the ark.

[24] And the waters prevailed on the earth 150 days.

[8:1] But God remembered Noah and all the beasts and all the livestock that were with him in the ark. And God made a wind blow over the earth, and the waters subsided.

[2] The fountains of the deep and the windows of the heavens were closed, the rain from the heavens was restrained,

[3] and the waters receded from the earth continually. At the end of 150 days the waters had abated,

[4] And in the seventh month, on the seventeenth day of

the month, the ark came to rest on the mountains of
Ararat.

[5] And the waters continued to abate until the tenth
month; in the tenth month, on the first day of the
month, the tops of the mountains were seen.

[6] At the end of forty days Noah opened the window of
the ark that he had made

[7] and sent forth a raven. It went to and fro until the
waters were dried up from the earth.

[8] Then he sent forth a dove from him, to see if the
waters had subsided from the face of the ground.

[9] But the dove found no place to set her foot, and she
returned to him to the ark, for the waters were still
on the face of the whole earth. So he put out his hand
and took her and brought her into the ark with him.

[10] He waited another seven days, and again he sent
forth the dove out of the ark.

[11] And the dove came back to him in the evening, and
behold, in her mouth was a freshly plucked olive leaf.
So Noah knew that the waters had subsided from the
earth.

[12] Then he waited another seven days and sent forth
the dove, and she did not return to him anymore.

[13] In the six hundred and first year, in the first month,
the first day of the month, the waters were dried from
off the earth. And Noah removed the covering of the
ark and looked, and behold, the face of the ground was
dry.

[14] In the second month, on the twenty-seventh day of the month, the earth had dried out.

[15] Then God said to Noah,

[16] "Go out from the ark, you and your wife, and your sons and your sons' wives with you.

[17] Bring out with you every living thing that is with you of all flesh—birds and animals and every creeping thing that creeps on the earth—that they may swarm on the earth, and be fruitful and multiply on the earth."

[18] So Noah went out, and his sons and his wife and his sons' wives with him.

[19] Every beast, every creeping thing, and every bird, everything that moves on the earth, went out by families from the ark.

[20] Then Noah built an altar to the LORD and took some of every clean animal and some of every clean bird and offered burnt offerings on the altar.

[21] And when the LORD smelled the pleasing aroma, the LORD said in his heart, "I will never again curse[a] the ground because of man, for the intention of man's heart is evil from his youth. Neither will I ever again strike down every living creature as I have done.

[22] While the earth remains, seedtime and harvest, cold and heat, summer and winter, day and night, shall not cease."

[9:1] And God blessed Noah and his sons and said to

them, "Be fruitful and multiply and fill the earth.

[2] The fear of you and the dread of you shall be upon every beast of the earth and upon every bird of the heavens, upon everything that creeps on the ground and all the fish of the sea. Into your hand they are delivered.

[3] Every moving thing that lives shall be food for you. And as I gave you the green plants, I give you everything.

4 But you shall not eat flesh with its life, that is, its blood.

[5] And for your lifeblood I will require a reckoning: from every beast I will require it and from man. From his fellow man I will require a reckoning for the life of man.

[6] "Whoever sheds the blood of man,
    by man shall his blood be shed,
for God made man in his own image.

[7] And you,[a] be fruitful and multiply, increase greatly on the earth and multiply in it."

[8] Then God said to Noah and to his sons with him, [9] "Behold, I establish my covenant with you and your offspring after you,

[10] and with every living creature that is with you, the birds, the livestock, and every beast of the earth with you, as many as came out of the ark; it is for every beast of the earth.

[11] I establish my covenant with you, that never again

shall all flesh be cut off by the waters of the flood, and
never again shall there be a flood to destroy the earth."

[12] And God said, "This is the sign of the covenant that
I make between me and you and every living creature
that is with you, for all future generations:

[13] I have set my bow in the cloud, and it shall be a sign
of the covenant between me and the earth.

[14] When I bring clouds over the earth and the bow is
seen in the clouds,

[15] I will remember my covenant that is between me
and you and every living creature of all flesh. And the
waters shall never again become a flood to destroy all
flesh.

[16] When the bow is in the clouds, I will see it and
remember the everlasting covenant between God and
every living creature of all flesh that is on the earth."

[17] God said to Noah, "This is the sign of the covenant
that I have established between me and all flesh that is
on the earth."

Hebrews 12: 27, 28
(Once More)

²⁷ This phrase, "Yet once more," indicates the removal of things that are shaken—that is, things that have been made—in order that the things that cannot be shaken may remain.

²⁸ Therefore let us be grateful for receiving a kingdom that cannot be shaken, and thus let us offer to God acceptable worship, with reverence and awe

About the Author

Ashley Lumpkin is a Georgia-raised, Carolina-based writer, editor, actor, and educator. She is the author of four poetry collections and is an award winning slam poet. She is one-fifth (and only Slytherin member) of the Big Dreams Collective. Above all else, Ashley considers herself a teacher, poet, and fryer of food. She is a lover of mathematics and language. She loves you too.

Other Books by Ashley

{} At First Sight

Terrorism and Other Topics for Tea

#AshleyLumpkin

I Hate You All Equally.